# THE WAY
## Walking in the Footsteps of Jesus
### *Youth Study Edition*

# The Way
## Walking in the Footsteps of Jesus

**Book**
*The Way*
978-1-4267-5251-3

**Devotional**
*The Way: 40 Days of Reflection*
978-1-4267-5252-0

**DVD**
*The Way: DVD with Leader Guide*
843504033033

**Youth Study**
*The Way: Youth Study Edition*
978-1-4267-5254-4

**Children's Study**
*The Way: Children's Leader Guide*
978-1-4267-5255-1

*For more information, visit* **www.AdamHamilton.org**.

---

## Also by Adam Hamilton

*The Journey*

*24 Hours That Changed the World*

*Forgiveness*

*Why?*

*When Christians Get It Wrong*

*Seeing Gray in a World of
   Black and White*

*Christianity's Family Tree*

*Selling Swimsuits in the Arctic*

*Christianity and World Religions*

*Confronting the Controversies*

*Making Love Last a Lifetime*

*Unleashing the Word*

*Leading Beyond the Walls*

*Final Words From the Cross*

# ADAM HAMILTON

# THE WAY
## Walking in the Footsteps of Jesus

Youth Study Edition
by Clare Golson Doyle

Foreword
by Jason Gant

ABINGDON PRESS
NASHVILLE

*The Way: Walking in the Footsteps of Jesus*

*Youth Study Edition*

*Copyright © 2012 by Abingdon Press*

All rights reserved.
No part of this work may be reproduced or transmitted in any form or by any means, electronic or mechanical, including photocopying and recording, or by any information storage or retrieval system, except as may be expressly permitted by the 1976 Copyright Act or in writing from the publisher. Requests for permission can be addressed to Permissions, The United Methodist Publishing House, P.O. Box 801, 201 Eighth Avenue South, Nashville, TN 37202-0801, or e-mailed to permissions@umpublishing.org.

*This book is printed on acid-free paper.*

ISBN 978-1-4267-5254-4

Scripture quotations marked CEB are from the Common English Bible. Copyright © 2011 by the Common English Bible. All rights reserved. Used by permission. www.CommonEnglishBible.com.

Scripture quotations marked NRSV are from the New Revised Standard Version of the Bible, copyright 1989, Division of Christian Education of the National Council of the Churches of Christ in the United States of America. Used by permission. All rights reserved.

12 13 14 15 16 17 18 19 20—10 9 8 7 6 5 4 3 2 1

MANUFACTURED IN THE UNITED STATES OF AMERICA

# Contents

# Foreword

"How cool is that?"

It's a common phrase from my senior pastor, Adam Hamilton, at The United Methodist Church of the Resurrection. Adam uses the phrase when talking about almost anything and everything he is passionate about: experiencing a joy-filled moment with his wife and daughters; uncovering a unique insight about Scripture; learning about nonbelievers who have confessed Christ as their personal Savior; or sharing historical and geographical learnings from his research and experience in the Holy Land.

Adam shared his learnings about the Holy Land most recently during Lent, when he preached a sermon series about Jesus' ministry. That series, featuring video footage taped on location, was the basis for his new book and study, *The Way: Walking in the Footsteps of Jesus*. In his sermon series, Adam invited and inspired our congregation to consider making a pilgrimage to the Holy Land once in our lifetimes. His challenge has sparked a movement across every age group of our congregation, young and old alike, to consider taking a walk where Jesus walked.

I had the honor of assisting Adam on a trip to the Holy Land and found my heart transformed through reading Scripture in the place where it was written. I wasn't the only one who was moved. A woman in her early eighties had wished her whole life to make that journey and walk where Jesus walked. Her husband was physically unable to join her on the trip, but she was determined to go. We hiked miles throughout the week, and she was right there with the group. When we arrived at the stations of the cross in Jerusalem, she was exhausted, and yet she was as excited as a teenage girl about walking the stations. She smiled from ear to ear. I assisted her in the walk, and as our spirits moved toward reverence and remembrance, she could no longer contain her emotions. Her tears flowed as I held her arm.

This past winter, as Adam was preparing to preach the series, our student ministries team began to contact and encourage all our teens and their families to be present in worship each weekend of Lent, leading up through Easter. We highlighted Adam's videos from the Holy Land, his new insights gained from the geography and archaeology of the area, and his new learnings from the Scriptures.

When the series began, the impact on our church was tremendous—especially among our students, and in particular on one high school student. He was in worship the first week, when Adam preached via video from the Holy Land. The footage showed an area of the Jordan River with limited access to visitors and tourists. When Adam entered the water to demonstrate and discuss baptism, something unexpected happened. Adam stopped preaching for a moment and exclaimed that the water was freezing—I mean *cold!* It shocked Adam, and we could see that he was suffering. There was sympathetic laughter from the congregation. Everyone felt for our senior pastor, who was willing that day to lead us by example.

Following the service, many of the comments were in response to the very human moment Adam had experienced in front of us all. Just then, the high school student came up to talk with me. He asked me about being baptized. He said he had never done it because his parents had wanted him to choose when he was ready. The student said, "If Adam could get into that freezing water on camera, then I can have the courage to give my life to Jesus. I know it sounds funny, but for me, it was God saying, 'What are you waiting for? I did this to show that I love you.'" God was at work, even in the humorous moment when our pastor waded into the cold, cold water!

Throughout this study, my hope and prayer is that you have moments like that: the smile from ear to ear, the flowing tears, the laughter of human connection, and the transformational power of the Holy Spirit.

You might even find yourself saying, "How cool is that?"

—Jason Gant, Director of Student Ministries
The United Methodist Church of the Resurrection

# Introduction

The most important story in the life of any Christian is the story of Jesus Christ. From his birth to his Resurrection, Jesus is the foundation of Christian faith and belief. The Gospels tell this inspiring story in four different ways, each from a unique and compelling perspective. All four Gospels spend considerable time telling about the ministry of Jesus here on earth. Those years of ministry are the primary focus of this study.

In the three short years he ministered, Jesus was able to teach us and to exemplify what it means to love God and to serve God. By studying where Jesus went and what he did in each place, we can learn about the path of discipleship and then walk in his footsteps.

We will look at his time at the Jordan River, where he was baptized; and in the wilderness, where he was tempted. We will explore Capernaum and the Sea of Galilee, places where he called his disciples and healed people. We will consider the importance of mountains in his life and what they mean for his disciples. We will see him calm the seas and spend time with the outcasts. And finally, we will follow Jesus as he goes to Jerusalem and faces the cross.

By walking in Jesus' footsteps, we can find strength, courage, and guidance for living as Christians. As we embark on this journey, may you grow in your love for Jesus and draw closer to him.

# Using This Book

Although this resource is intended for teens, the book itself is set up like an adult Bible study. Whether a leader or a participant, everyone has the same book and literally is on the same page. Leaders should review the material in advance to determine which activities and discussion questions the group will use.

The book includes six sessions plus an epilogue, making it ideal for the season of Lent (one session for each Sunday during Lent, plus an optional session for Easter Sunday). However, the impact of Jesus' ministry is not limited to a certain time of year. Regardless of the season, this study is a great way for youth classes or Bible study groups to get a better understanding of where Jesus walked and what Jesus taught. And by studying his ministry, we can learn more about how to live as Christians today.

Each of the sessions includes the following parts:

*Goals for This Session*—Each session identifies a few goals. These goals give leaders some clear teaching objectives and participants something to focus on as they walk in the footsteps of Jesus.

*Words to Know*—Readers are given definitions of key words and place-names that may be unfamiliar to them.

*Introduction*—While it is impossible to walk with Jesus physically, we can draw closer to him by studying the places he went and the message he taught. Every session's introduction makes a connection between a place Jesus visited, the message Jesus taught there, and situations most young people face in daily life. Group members can read the introduction prior to each session, or groups can spend time reading during each session.

*Biblical Foundation*—The best accounts of Jesus' travel and ministry are found in the four Gospels. So the foundation of each session is a text from one of the four Gospels that tells the story of Jesus' ministry.

*Video Presentation and Discussion*—Your group may be interested in the optional yet recommended DVD that goes with this program. In it, Adam Hamilton leads viewers to sites throughout the Holy Land, describing what took place at each location and why it is important. Each segment is about 10 minutes. This book provides a list of key sights and insights for each segment, along with a list of discussion questions.

*Bringing the Scripture to My Life*—One of the main objectives of this study is to help participants make connections between the ministry of Jesus and their lives today. This part of each session provides discussion questions that help make those connections.

*Going Deeper in Truth*—While the biblical foundation of every session is taken from one of the Gospels, other Scriptures can also give us insight into the significance of Jesus' ministry and what we can learn from his teachings.

*Experiencing Life in Community*—Jesus and his closest followers were a tight-knit community. They traveled together, ate together, learned together, and were in ministry together. Those who follow Jesus have maintained this emphasis on community, and life in community is an important part of each session.

*Making It Personal*—Belonging to a community of believers is an essential part of the Christian life, but the gospel also has a significant influence on us as individuals. Every session gives instructions for individuals to put what they've learned into action during the coming week.

*Listening for God*—Every session concludes with a time of prayer and reflection, lifting up what the participants have learned and asking God's guidance as everyone goes forth.

This book is about walking in the footsteps of Jesus, not just in the Holy Land but in our daily lives. If Christ set the oppressed free, delivered people from their demons, and brought healing to the sick and wounded, what does that mean for us as his followers?

—From *The Way: Walking in the Footsteps of Jesus,*
   by Adam Hamilton

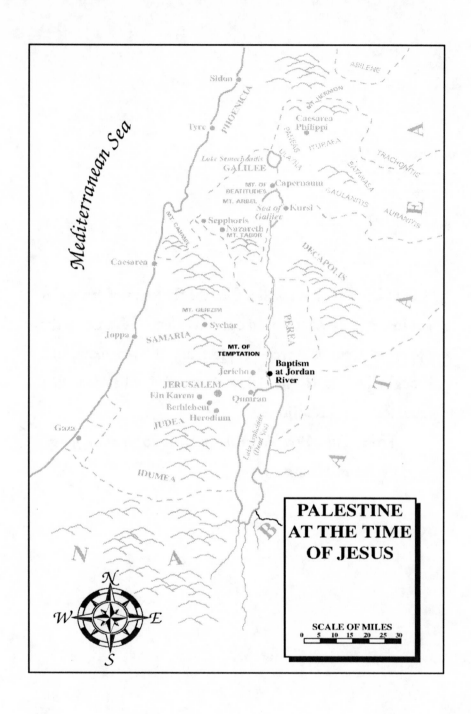

**PALESTINE AT THE TIME OF JESUS**

SCALE OF MILES

0    5    10    15    20    25    30

# 1. Baptism and Temptation
## *The Jordan River and the Wilderness*

# Getting Started

## *Goals for This Session*

—Explore Jesus' baptism in the Jordan River and temptation in the wilderness.

—Understand that temptation comes to all people.

—Recognize that following Jesus can give strength in times of temptation.

## *Words to Know*

**Baptism:** This word comes from the Greek word *baptisma*. It is a sacrament in the church and is a sign of purification or cleansing and signifies that one is a part of the family of God.

**Temptation:** This word comes from the Greek word *peirazo*. It means testing. To resist temptation means to pass the test or turn away from doing something that is wrong.

# Introduction

Temptations! Temptations are around us all the time. They are everywhere. Small and large temptations can stare you in the face every day. From the time we are children, we are warned about temptations, but as we grow, the temptations get bigger and can have significant consequences. Lying, cheating, drugs, sex, alcohol, and gossip are just a few of the temptations that seem to be part of life.

Think about the temptations you face daily.
- What are the temptations?
- If you give in to them, what are the consequences?
- How do you overcome them?
- Where do you find the strength to face them down?

Jesus knew all about temptations and how to fight them. And if you walk in his footsteps, you can find strength to face the temptations in your own life. Jesus knew what it was like to be tempted. He faced them in his own life. But something else happened first, and it was right at the beginning of his ministry. Jesus went to the Jordan River and was baptized by his cousin John.

Jesus' baptism showed that he was beloved of God, just as baptism is a powerful symbol for all Christians. When we face tough times—and we can be sure that we will—we can remember that we are beloved of God.

But baptism was only the beginning. Immediately after Jesus was baptized in the Jordan River, he went into the wilderness for forty days and forty nights. There he was tempted. He was tormented. His identity as the Son of God was questioned. He was challenged to skip the pain and the agony of the cross and was tempted to sell himself for wealth and power. These temptations come to all of us in some form or another. Because Jesus was able to face the temptations, so can we. It is not easy. Jesus spent time in prayer and focusing on God. If we do the same, we will find strength.

# Exploring the Lesson

## Biblical Foundation

In those days Jesus came from Nazareth of Galilee and was baptized by John in the Jordan. And just as he was coming up out of the water, he saw the heavens torn apart and the Spirit descending like a dove on him. And a voice came from heaven, "You are my Son, the Beloved; with you I am well pleased." And the Spirit immediately drove him out into the wilderness. He was in the wilderness forty days, tempted by Satan; and he was with the wild beasts; and the angels waited on him. (Mark 1:9-13 NRSV)

## Video Presentation and Discussion (Optional)

On the DVD, watch Session 1: Baptism and Temptation.

SIGHTS
- Qumran is the place where John the Baptist spent years studying and worshiping.
- A *mikvah* was a place of ritual baths.
- The Jordan River was where Jesus was baptized.
- The Mount of Temptation was the place in the wilderness where Jesus was thought to have spent forty days being tempted by Satan.

INSIGHTS

Jesus chose to be baptized by John, and it marked the beginning of his ministry. Immediately after this great experience he went into the wilderness and was tempted. Jesus' baptism prepared him for what was to come. Like Jesus' baptism, all Christian baptisms mark new beginnings and can offer strength to overcome temptation.

- How can seeing where Jesus was baptized help you?
- What are some ways that baptism, or the stories of it, can help us in our lives?

The very next place where Jesus headed was into the wilderness. On the Mount of Temptation there is a cave. Imagine Jesus sleeping in the cave, wandering in the wilderness, and facing the temptations presented to him.

- How can seeing the barrenness and desolation of the cave and the wilderness where Jesus was tempted help you when you face temptation?
- What types of temptation have you faced in your life, and how did you respond?
- Does it help to know that Jesus understands how you feel in the midst of temptations? How?

## *Bringing the Scripture to My Life*

Seeing where Jesus was baptized and tempted can be a very powerful reminder of how to face life with strength and courage. Through baptism, followers of Jesus Christ participate in his life, death, and Resurrection. It doesn't mean our lives will be perfect or that we will not sin, but through baptism God can help you to lead a better life.

For Jesus, his baptism was a defining act. In that moment, he identified with sinners and heard God's affirmation that he was the Father's beloved son. He received the Spirit's power. And, it marked the beginning of his ministry. Jesus' baptism was an ordination in which he was set aside and empowered for his mission of drawing people to God inviting them into God's kingdom, demonstrating God's will, and ultimately laying down his life for humanity.

For us, as Christ's followers, baptism is also meant as a defining act. Through our baptism we are claimed by God, anointed with the Spirit, and set aside for God's purposes. Our brokenness is recognized and God's grace is promised. And in our baptisms we are initiated into, and become a part of, God's covenant people. We are meant to remember our baptisms each day. Even if we don't remember the act itself, we remember that God has promised to forgive our sins, that we are called to ministry that the Holy Spirit resides in us, and that we are God's children.

—From *The Way: Walking in the Footsteps of Jesus*, by Adam Hamilton

## *Going Deeper in Truth*

Read Matthew 26:41 (CEB)
"Stay alert and pray so that you won't give in to temptation. The spirit is eager, but the flesh is weak."

- What does it mean when Jesus says the spirit is willing, but the flesh is weak?
- Is it hard to pray when you are in the middle of a trial or temptation?
- How do you think prayer can help?

Read Matthew 6:13 (CEB)

"And don't lead us into temptation, but rescue us from the evil one."

- How do you feel evil in your life?
- From what temptations do you need to be delivered?

Read 1 Corinthians 10:13 (CEB)

No temptation has seized you that isn't common for people. But God is faithful. He won't allow you to be tempted beyond your abilities. Instead, with the temptation, God will also supply a way out so that you will be able to endure it.

- How has God been faithful to you when you were being tempted?
- How can you help someone who is being tempted?

## *Experiencing Life in Community*

Discuss the idea, practice, and meaning of baptism. Talk about the different ways people can be baptized, such as sprinkling, pouring, or immersion, and about some of the differences among infant, youth, and adult baptism. Then take a bowl of water and pass it from person to person and let them dip their fingers into the water, remembering Jesus' baptism in the Jordan River and, if appropriate, their own baptism. Before you pass the bowl, offer this prayer:

*Dear God, as we look at this water and touch it with our fingers, help us to recall Jesus' baptism. Help us to remember that all of us have been washed by your grace and that we are your children. Fill us with your Spirit and help us to live each day as faithful followers of Jesus Christ. Amen.*

## *Making It Personal*

Here are two ways to put what you've learned into action in the coming week and beyond:

1. Spend time reflecting on baptism. Think about what it means to be a child of God. If you were baptized as an infant, ask your family about your baptism. If you haven't been baptized, think about ways your life might be changed day to day if you were.

2. List all the people in your life who you know are facing temptations. Spend time each day praying for the people on your list. Ask God to give them strength.

# Wrapping Up

## *Listening for God*

Gather as a group for prayer. Each person should think about the temptations that are faced in daily life. Think about how Jesus would have handled the temptations. Close the session by giving thanks to God for sending Jesus so he can show us the way in our lives.

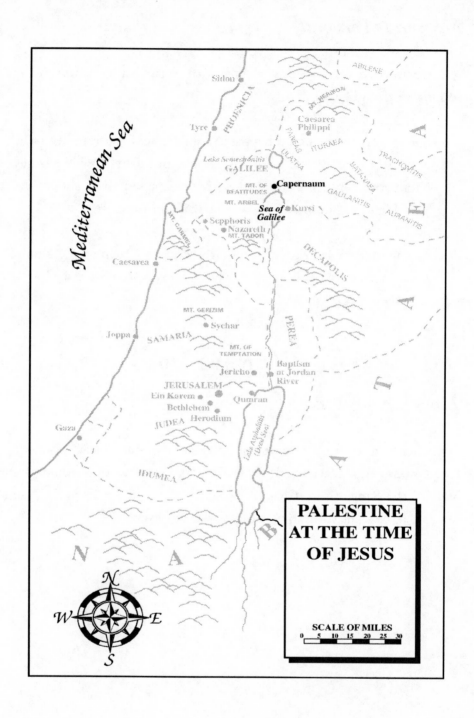

Mediterranean Sea

ABILENE

Sidon

PHOENICIA

MT. HERMON

Tyre

Caesarea
Philippi

PANEAS
ITURAEA

ULATHA

TRACHONITIS

Lake Semechonitis

GALILEE

BATANAEA

MT. OF
BEATITUDES

Capernaum

GAULANITIS

MT. ARBEL

AURANITIS

Sea of
Galilee

Kursi

MT. CARMEL

Sepphoris

Nazareth

MT. TABOR

DECAPOLIS

Caesarea

MT. GERIZIM

Sychar

PEREA

Joppa

SAMARIA

MT. OF
TEMPTATION

Jericho

Baptism
at Jordan
River

JERUSALEM

Ein Karem

Bethlehem

Qumran

Gaza

JUDEA

Herodium

Lake Asphaltitis
(Dead Sea)

IDUMEA

NABA

**PALESTINE
AT THE TIME
OF JESUS**

N

A

B

N

W

E

S

**SCALE OF MILES**

0   5   10   15   20   25   30

# 2. The Healing Ministry
## *Capernaum*

# Getting Started

## *Goals for This Session*

—Explore the Gospel stories of how Jesus healed people.
—Understand that Jesus still heals today.
—Recognize that Jesus needs stretcher-bearers to help in his healing ministry.

## *Words to Know*

**Healing:** This word means to become whole or healthy.

**Stretcher-Bearer:** In this chapter, a stretcher-bearer is one who is willing to bring a friend to Jesus for healing.

# Introduction

Look at the world around you. Does it seem to be in good shape? There are definitely some good things in the world, but there are also things that are not so good. Some obvious problems involve our physical health, for example:

- Cancer
- Multiple sclerosis
- Parkinson's disease
- Injuries due to traumatic events

There is a great need for healing in our world. It is true today and it was true in Jesus' day. After Jesus was baptized and tempted, he returned to his hometown of Nazareth. There he was not well received, and his own people sent him away. So he wandered along the Sea of Galilee. As he traveled he began to heal people. Eventually he made his way to the town of Capernaum. There, Jesus taught in the synagogue, preached the good news, and healed hundreds of people.

What kind of healing did he do? Jesus healed people of their physical illnesses, and the Scriptures say he "cast out demons." These demons may have been what we now know to be neurological disorders or psychiatric illnesses. They may have been evil voices or temptations that people could not overcome on their own. Regardless of the causes, Jesus brought healing and deliverance to the people around him.

Jesus came to save the world, to heal the broken and the sick. The Scriptures tell us that he called the disciples to help him. Besides the disciples, Jesus had other helpers, whom today we sometimes refer to as "stretcher-bearers," people who carried their friends to receive healing from Jesus. Jesus said the healing took place not so much because of the friends' faith, but because of the stretcher-bearers' faith.

Who are your stretcher-bearers? For whom can you be a stretcher-bearer?

# Exploring the Lesson

## *Biblical Foundation*

Now when Jesus heard that John had been arrested, he withdrew to Galilee. He left Nazareth and made his home in Capernaum by the sea. (Matthew 4:12-13 NRSV)

They went to Capernaum; and when the Sabbath came, he entered the synagogue and taught. They were astounded at his teaching, for he taught them as one having authority, and not as the scribes. Just then there was in their synagogue a man with an unclean spirit, and he cried out, "What have you to do with us, Jesus of Nazareth? Have you come to destroy us? I know who you are, the Holy One of God." But Jesus rebuked him, saying, "Be silent, and come out of him!" (Mark 1:21-25 NRSV)

As soon as they left the synagogue, they entered the house of Simon and Andrew, with James and John. Now Simon's mother-in-law was in bed with a fever, and they told him about her at once. He came and took her by the hand and lifted her up. Then the fever left her, and she began to serve them. That evening, at sundown, they brought to him all who were sick or possessed with demons. (Mark 1:29-32 NRSV)

# Video Presentation and Discussion (Optional)

On the DVD, watch Session 2: The Healing Ministry.

## SIGHTS

- The site of the synagogue in Nazareth
- The Sea of Galilee
- The town of Capernaum
- The synagogue in Capernaum
- The home of Peter, where Jesus healed Peter's mother as well as many others, including the paralyzed man whose friends lowered him through the roof

## INSIGHTS

Jesus first went to Nazareth, the town where he had grown up, to proclaim his identity and begin his ministry. However, he was rejected by the townspeople. He left Nazareth and traveled along the Sea of Galilee, toward the town of Capernaum.

- How do you think Jesus felt as he walked away from Nazareth?
- How does seeing the seashore along the Sea of Galilee help you to focus on Jesus' ministry?

As Jesus walked, he began to heal people. When he arrived in Capernaum, he taught at synagogue and healed many, many people.

- What does it mean for your life to see the places where Jesus walked, talked, preached, and healed?
- When you see the remains of the house where the paralyzed man was lowered to Jesus for healing, how does it help you imagine what happened?

- What effect can you have on another person's healing?
- Who has helped to carry you when you were sick?

## Bringing the Scripture to My Life

Throughout the Gospels there are multiple stories of Jesus casting out demons, forgiving sins, and healing people. Jesus had deep compassion for those who were sick. He also healed those who had spiritual or psychological problems, such as guilt or shame. As we read about the healings, we learn that we are all in need of stretcher-bearers.

Jesus still heals hearts. He still forgives sins. He still heals our bodies, casts out demons, and sets people free. And we still need stretcher-bearers, people who will carry us and pray for us and have faith for us when our own faith is weak or nonexistent.

—From *The Way: Walking in the Footsteps of Jesus*, by Adam Hamilton

## Going Deeper in Truth

Read Luke 5:18-19 (CEB)
Some men were bringing a man who was paralyzed, lying on a cot. They wanted to carry him in and place him before Jesus, but they couldn't reach him because of the crowd. So they took him up on the roof and lowered him—cot and all—through the roof tiles into the crowded room in front of Jesus.

- What does it mean to have Jesus forgive sin?
- What sins do you need to have forgiven so that you can be healed?

Read Acts 5:14-16 (CEB)
Indeed, more and more believers in the Lord, large numbers of both men and women, were added to the church. As a result, they would even

bring the sick out into the main streets and lay them on cots and mats so that at least Peter's shadow could fall on some of them as he passed by. Even large numbers of persons from towns around Jerusalem would gather, bringing the sick and those harassed by unclean spirits. Everyone was healed.

- How does it make you feel, knowing that the disciples were able to heal the sick after Jesus died, rose, and ascended into heaven?
- How do you think Jesus can use you to heal others?

Read Matthew 25:36-37, 39 (CEB)

"'I was sick and you took care of me. I was in prison and you visited me.' Then those who are righteous will reply to him, 'Lord, . . . when did we see you sick or in prison and visit you?'"

- Who cares for you when you are sick?
- How does it make you feel to have others caring for you?
- What does it mean that when we care for the sick, we are caring for Jesus?

## Experiencing Life in Community

### STRETCHER-BEARER RELAY

Set up a relay course with obstacles of chairs, cushions, tables, and other objects. At the end of the course, put a cross. Divide into two equal teams. Teams must choose one person to be the friend, and the rest of the team will be stretcher-bearers. At a signal, the teams will work together to carry the friend through the obstacle course to the cross. Afterward, discuss how it felt to be the friend and how it felt to be a stretcher-bearer.

### HELPING THE STRETCHER-BEARERS

Make a list of groups in your community who are stretcher-bearers. The list might include nurses, firefighters, and police. Think of ways you could help these groups. For instance, you might hold a toy drive so police can have toys for children who have experienced abuse. You might plan games to play with seniors at your local nursing home. You might bake cookies and take them to the fire station. Think of many different ideas; then select one activity that your group will do.

## *Making It Personal*

This week, identify the people around you who are sick, who are addicted to some bad behavior, or who need the healing of Jesus in their lives. For each person, make a paper chain loop and link these together. You may add links as you see or learn of someone else who needs healing. Use your chain to pray each day that the people will find healing.

# Wrapping Up

## *Listening for God*

Have the group stand in a circle. Each person, if willing, should take a turn standing in the middle. Each time, the group will place their hands on the person in the middle and silently pray for him or her. Close with this prayer:

> *O God, we pray for each other today. Help each one of us here. Touch the parts of our lives that need healing and help us touch the lives of those around us who need to be healed. Go with us now so that, as your followers, we may be your hands and feet in the world. Amen.*

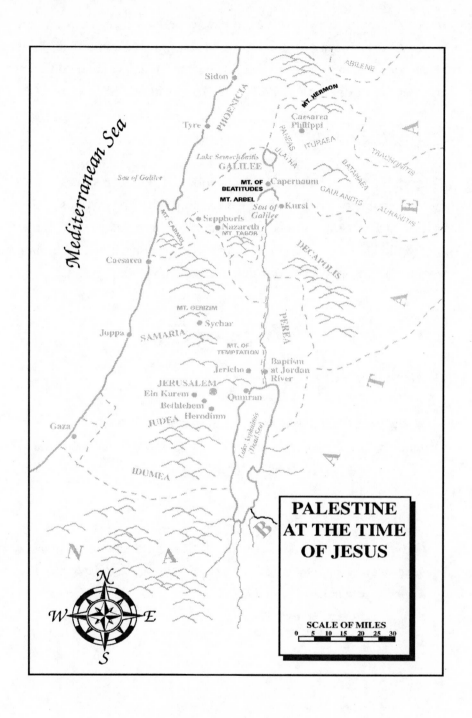

Mediterranean Sea

ABILENE

Sidon

MT. HERMON

Tyre

PHOENICIA

Caesarea
Philippi

PANEAS

ITURAEA

TRACHONITIS

Lake Semechonitis

ULATHA

BATANEA

GALILEE

Sea of Galilee

MT. OF
BEATITUDES

Capernaum

GAULANITIS

AURANITIS

MT. ARBEL

Sea of
Galilee

Kursi

Sepphoris

Nazareth

MT. TABOR

DECAPOLIS

Caesarea

MT. GERIZIM

PEREA

Joppa

Sychar

SAMARIA

MT. OF
TEMPTATION

Jericho

Baptism
at Jordan
River

JERUSALEM

Ein Karem

Bethlehem

Qumran

Herodium

JUDEA

Gaza

Lake Asphaltitis
(Dead Sea)

IDUMEA

N          A

N

W          E

S

## PALESTINE
## AT THE TIME
## OF JESUS

SCALE OF MILES

0    5    10   15   20   25   30

# 3. Proclaiming the Kingdom
## *The Mountains*

## Getting Started

### *Goals for This Session*

—Get a sense of the importance of mountains in Jesus' life and ours.
—Understand that places of solitude offer us quiet time with God and strength to face our daily lives.
—Recognize that by loving others we are loving God.

### *Words to Know*

**Repent:** This word comes from a Greek word that means to change one's mind. In the Christian faith it means to stop, turn around, and do something differently.

***Kalos:*** This is a Greek word that means "for good." It means that actions are beautiful and attract others by setting an example.

## *Introduction*

Think about times in your life when you have felt exhilarated. Perhaps you had the feeling at the conclusion of church camp or after a mission trip or a youth retreat. Life is great. Life is good. You are on top of the world and can handle anything that comes your way. And then, daily life settles in. You have homework to finish, papers to write, tests to study for, chores to do.

How do you recapture those feelings of peace and contentment? You find places or activities that help you face daily life. Jesus knew that all of us need places to go in order to restore our balance.

Jesus had such places. Often, they were the mountains. He rested on mountains, he prayed on mountains, he struggled on mountains. He seemed to find peace on mountains talking with God. Mountains seemed to give him courage and strength to face the difficult parts of his life.

It is important to find places where you can go to spend time alone with God. These places can help you to talk to God, listen to God, and hear God. Your place might be at your home or a park, or even a church where you can just be quiet. Your place may not be a physical location but anywhere you can reflect on Scripture or listen to a song. Your place may be very different from another person's. What is important is that you can use it to talk to God and listen to God. If you spend time with God and truly listen, you may find that you need to repent, or live differently. Perhaps you'll discover that you need to act in a new way.

- Describe a time when you felt especially close to God.
- How can such an experience help you to live like Jesus and give you strength and courage for your daily life?

After going to the mountains, Jesus returned to daily life. For example, after teaching from a mountain in the Sermon on the Mount, he came down and showed us how to live in daily life. Through his actions, Jesus taught us how to love one another, how to be kind and caring without being judgmental, and how, by loving others, we are also loving him.

- What are some ways in which you can give back to Jesus some of the love you have experienced?
- Name some ways to love your neighbor—not next week or next year, but today.

# Exploring the Lesson

## Biblical Foundation

When Jesus saw the crowds, he went up the mountain; and after he sat down, his disciples came to him. Then he began to speak, and taught them. . . . (Matthew 5:1-2 NRSV)

## Video Presentation and Discussion (Optional)

On the DVD, watch Session 3: Proclaiming the Kingdom.

SIGHTS
- Mount Arbel near the Sea of Galilee is one of the places where Jesus went for prayers, fasting, teaching, and guidance.
- The Mount of Beatitudes is the location where Jesus preached one of his most beloved messages.

INSIGHTS

There are many mountains talked about in the Gospels. In fact, mountains are mentioned twenty-nine times. Mountains were important to Jesus. Adam Hamilton imagines Jesus on a mountain, praying and looking out over the places and people of his ministry.

- Why do you think mountains are such a good place to pray and think?
- In what ways does it help to see things from a great height?

When Jesus came down from the mountains, he called for us to repent.
- What does it mean to repent?
- Have there been times for you when repentance was hard? when it didn't seem to help? How did you feel, and what did you do?

## *Bringing the Scripture to My Life*

Jesus went up to the mountains for important times in life. Are you better able to share God's love with others when you spend time with God?

In the Sermon on the Mount, Jesus teaches us how we should live and how we should seek to serve others. Our actions are to set examples, to be *kalos* for others, bringing them closer to God.

> Are your deeds winsome and beautiful to others? . . . May your life, and our churches, be characterized by beautiful deeds, flowing from hearts of compassion and love that draw others into the Kingdom.
> —From *The Way: Walking in the Footsteps of Jesus*, by Adam Hamilton

## *Going Deeper in Truth*

Read Ephesians 6:24 (NRSV)

Grace be with all who have an undying love for our Lord Jesus Christ.

- How can you have an undying love for God?
- What does an undying love for God look like?

Read Hebrews 13:1-2 (CEB)

Keep loving each other like family. Don't neglect to open up your homes to guests, because by doing this some have been hosts to angels without knowing it.

- What does it mean to love each other "like family"?
- What is an angel? Who have you helped who might have been an angel?

Read John 13:35 (CEB)

"This is how everyone will know that you are my disciples, when you love each other."

- What does it mean to you to be a disciple of Jesus?
- When Jesus said we should love each other, what kinds of actions do you think he had in mind?

## *Experiencing Life in Community*

### MAKE A WEB OF CONNECTEDNESS

Form a circle. In the center of the circle place a table or chair with a Bible in it. Tie the end of a ball of string to the Bible, then have the leader toss the ball of string to one person in the group. Have this person hold onto the string, then toss the ball of string to someone else in the circle. Continue this action until everyone in the group is holding onto the string, and a web has been formed connecting each member to each other and to the Bible. Talk about how it is important for us to stay connected to one another and to God.

### DESIGN A BUMPER STICKER

Pass out sheets of paper the size of a bumper sticker. Work as individuals or in groups to design a bumper sticker that tells who you are as a Christian and what you believe. If you are willing, present your bumper sticker to the group. Talk about how it expresses who you are as you walk in the footsteps of Jesus.

## Making It Personal

Here are two ways to put what you've learned into action in the coming week and beyond:

1. Find a quiet place where you can spend time with God. Tell God what is going on in your life. Listen for what God is calling you to do.

2. Look around you each day. Find someone who needs to be loved. It may be someone who is having a hard time in school and needs a word of encouragement. It may be someone who needs a friend. It may be a neighbor who is hurting. When you have found someone, act toward him or her in a loving and caring way.

# Wrapping Up

## *Listening for God*

Close your eyes. Imagine that you are on your mountain, wherever that may be. Think about how you got there. Feel the calm of being there. Let the presence of God enter your heart. Listen for your heartbeat, and feel the movement of God in your life with each beat. Think about how good that feels. Imagine ways you can pass that feeling on to others. Slowly open your eyes. Commit to passing on the love of God every day this week.

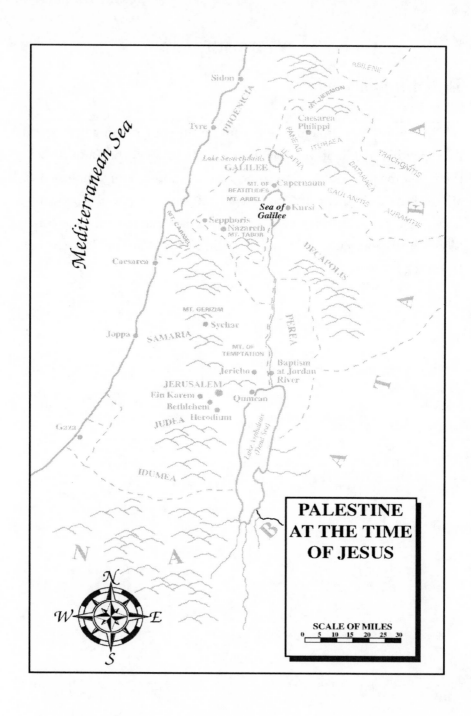

Mediterranean Sea

Sidon

PHOENICIA

Tyre

ABILENE

MT. HERMON

Caesarea
Philippi

PANEAS ITURAEA

ULATHA

TRACHONITIS

Lake Semechonitis

GALILEE

BATANAEA

MT. OF
BEATITUDES
Capernaum

MT. ARBEL

GAULANITIS

AURANITIS

Sepphoris

Sea of
Galilee

Kursi

Nazareth

MT. TABOR

DECAPOLIS

Caesarea

MT. GERIZIM

Sychar

SAMARIA

PEREA

Joppa

MT. OF
TEMPTATION

Baptism
at Jordan
River

Jericho

JERUSALEM

Ein Karem

Qumran

Bethlehem

Herodium

JUDEA

Lake Asphaltus (Dead Sea)

Gaza

IDUMEA

N A B A T A

N

A

**PALESTINE
AT THE TIME
OF JESUS**

N

W        E

S

**SCALE OF MILES**
0    5    10   15   20   25   30

# 4. Calming the Storm
## *The Sea of Galilee*

# Getting Started

## *Goals for This Session*

—Understand that Jesus calls us.
—Begin to recognize how Jesus can calm the storms of our lives.
—Get an understanding that Jesus truly is the Son of God.

## *Words to Know*

**Nave:** This is a Latin word that means ship. The nave is the central part of the church sanctuary. In modern sanctuaries, this where the congregation sits.

***Ego eimi:*** This is a two-word Greek phrase that means *I Am* or *It Is I*. In the Old Testament, the Hebrew form of these words would have been Yahweh or Jehovah.

## Introduction

The weather forecast calls for severe weather. Storms, hail, hurricanes, and blizzards are bearing down. An earthquake triggers a tsunami. A volcano spews lava. Storms can be terrifying and drastically change people's lives. But weather is not the only type of storm that can enter life. Difficult, dark times can enter our lives at any moment.

You can be having a normal day, and then *wham!* You get a call that something has happened. You may have lost a friend in a car wreck. A grandparent may have passed away. Your dad or mom may have lost a job. There are many storms that can change our lives. Jesus knew all about this.

- Are you in the midst of a storm?
- Who around you is in the midst of a storm?

Jesus found his first disciples on the water. He came into their lives, called them to follow, and they said "yes." Like those first disciples, we are called by Jesus. All we have to do is to say, "Yes, I will follow." Jesus helps us do the rest.

- What do you think Jesus was doing that day at the Sea of Galilee when he met the first disciples?
- Do you go to the water? What do you do there? How does it make you feel?

That day, Jesus brought peace in the midst of the storm. There is a lesson in this for today, since at times all of us will face a situation that terrifies us. It may be an illness that strikes us or someone dear to us. It could be divorce, an extended period of unemployment, or any number of other things. Individually and collectively, we will face strong winds and huge waves in the middle of night with no life jackets. In those moments, Jesus wants us to remember that if we invite him, he will always be in the boat with us. —From *The Way: Walking in the Footsteps of Jesus*, by Adam Hamilton

# Exploring the Lesson

## *Biblical Foundation*

On that day, when evening had come, he said to them, "Let us go across to the other side." And leaving the crowd behind, they took him with them in the boat, just as he was. Other boats were with him. A great windstorm arose, and the waves beat into the boat, so that the boat was already being swamped. But he was in the stern, asleep on the cushion; and they woke him up and said to him, "Teacher, do you not care that we are perishing?" He woke up and rebuked the wind, and said to the sea. "Peace! Be still!" Then the wind ceased, and there was a dead calm. He said to them, "Why are you afraid? Have you still no faith?" And they were filled with great awe and said to one another "Who then is this, that even the wind and the sea obey him?" (Mark 4:35-41 NRSV)

## *Video Presentation and Discussion (Optional)*

On the DVD, watch Session 4: Calming the Storm.

SIGHTS

- The Sea of Galilee is the lowest freshwater lake in the world and the largest freshwater body in the Holy Land. The Jordan River flows in and out of it.
- The fisherman named Yaeri demonstrates how to fish with a net. He tells us something about the nature of fishermen and talks about Jesus.

INSIGHTS

The Gospels mention boats forty-three times. Since water and boats were important in the ministry of Jesus, it is important for us to examine the stories and see their relevance for our lives.

- What did you think about or learn from seeing a modern-day fisherman on the Sea of Galilee?
- How does it make you feel to know that even Jesus' disciples got scared? When have you been scared, and how did you respond?

The Gospel accounts tell us that Jesus calmed the wind and waves and that he walked on water.

- How did the disciples respond? What do you think they learned?
- What did you learn? What questions do you have?

## *Bringing the Scripture to My Life*

Jesus called the disciples in the midst of their everyday lives. He comes to us, too, in the midst of what we are doing.

Even when Jesus was with the disciples in a boat, they were scared of the storm. When we are frightened, we need to look to Jesus, as the disciples did.

Scripture, tradition, and even the architecture of many churches communicate the image of Jesus calming the storms. The nave ("ship"), where we sit in worship, reminds us that God is our captain. Through water, Jesus revealed his identity. When the disciples saw him walk on water, they were afraid, and he said to them, "It is I."

In that moment, Jesus demonstrated that he was Lord over the forces of the deep, and over the wind and the rain. The scene takes us back to that moment when Moses parted the waters of the Red Sea. Jesus had that kind of power over nature, and the disciples realized once again that they were not dealing with an ordinary man.

—From *The Way: Walking in the Footsteps of Jesus*, by Adam Hamilton

## Going Deeper in Truth

Read Psalm 29:11 (CEB)
Let the LORD give strength to his people!
Let the LORD bless his people with peace!
- When have you needed strength?
- How does it feel to be blessed?
- How can you be a blessing to someone else?

Read John 14:27 (CEB)
"Peace I leave with you. My peace I give you. I give to you not as the world gives. Don't be troubled or afraid."
- When have you needed peace? How did you respond?
- What does it mean to you not to be troubled or afraid?

Read Psalm 107:28-29 (CEB)
So they cried out to the LORD in their distress,
and God brought them out safe from their desperate circumstances.
God quieted the storm to a whisper;
the sea's waves were hushed.
- Where do you need Christ's calming presence in your life?
- What does it mean to have Christ with you in the storms of life?

## Experiencing Life in Community

### Who Is in the Midst of a Storm?

Select pictures of people from magazines who look upset. Place these around the room. Each person should choose a picture. Imagine why that person is upset. Then think about a way Jesus could help him or her. Present your thoughts to the group.

### Newscast

Divide into two groups. Each group is to be a news station with the task of presenting a newscast. Group one is to report on Jesus walking on the water. Group two is to report on a modern-day event where Jesus has come to someone in the middle of a storm. Present the newscasts to the full group.

## Making It Personal

Here are two ways to put what you've learned into action in the coming week and beyond:

1. Get a long sheet of paper, or tape several pieces of paper together horizontally. Draw a long horizontal line on the paper—a timeline of your life. Above the line, list the important events of your life. Below the line, list the times when you needed Jesus the most and felt his presence in your life. Think about how Jesus is with you when life is calm and when life is stormy. Use your timeline to remember that Jesus is always with you.

2. Think about someone you have seen in your daily life, whom you don't know but who appears to be struggling. Then write the conclusion to this story.

The other day, I saw someone who was having a really hard time. I think there might be a storm in their life. I think knowing about Jesus could help.

I am going to help them by saying _____.

Then I am going help them by doing _____.

# Wrapping Up

## *Listening for God*

Play some quiet, reflective music. Place a cross in the middle of the group. Spend time thinking about the stormy times in your life. On the adhesive side of a sticky note, write about a storm you are facing. Each person is to stick their note on the cross. Spend some time thinking about how Jesus loves each of us enough to be with us even when times are tough. Close with this prayer.

> *Dear God, thank you for being with us in good times and bad. Please help us feel your presence when the storms of life are raging. Amen.*

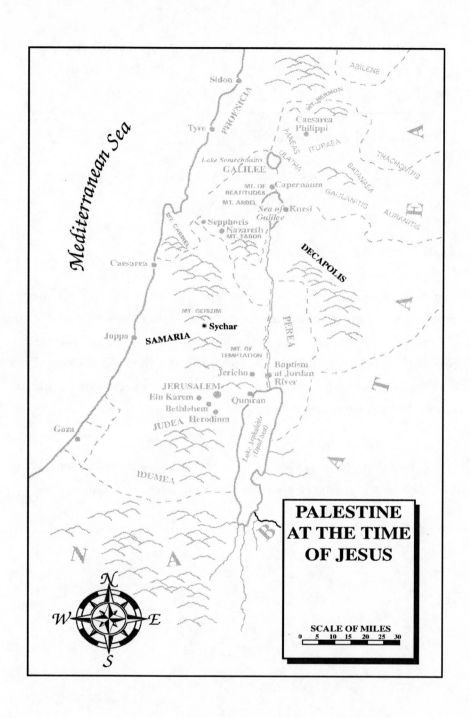

Mediterranean Sea

ABILENE

Sidon

PHOENICIA

MT. HERMON

Caesarea
Philippi

Tyre

ITURAEA

PANEAS

ULATHA

TRACHONITIS

Lake Semechonitis

GALILEE

BATANEA

MT. OF
BEATITUDES

Capernaum

GAULANITIS

MT. ARBEL

AURANITIS

Sea of
Galilee

Kursi

MT. CARMEL

Sepphoris
Nazareth
MT. TABOR

DECAPOLIS

Caesarea

MT. GERIZIM

● Sychar

SAMARIA

PEREA

Joppa

MT. OF
TEMPTATION

Jericho

Baptism
at Jordan
River

JERUSALEM

Ein Karem

Bethlehem

Qumran

Gaza

JUDEA

Herodium

Lake Asphaltitis
(Dead Sea)

IDUMEA

N

A

B

A

T

A

E

A

## PALESTINE
## AT THE TIME
## OF JESUS

N

W        E

S

**SCALE OF MILES**
0   5   10   15   20   25   30

# 5. Sinners, Outcasts, and the Poor
## *Samaria*

## Getting Started

### *Goals for This Session*

—Explore some of the stories about how Jesus cared for society's outcasts.

—Understand that following Jesus means caring for people who are not accepted by others.

—Recognize that there are multiple ways to care for sinners, outcasts, and the poor.

### *Words to Know*

**Am ha-aretz:** This word is a derogatory term from the Hebrew language, used to mean the lower classes of people, the ignorant, the unfaithful, or the outcasts of society.

**Samaritans:** This word refers to a group of people from the area called Samaria. In Jesus' time, Samaritans were shunned by Israelites.

# *Introduction*

Jesus often used stories or parables to teach. Here is a story for you to consider:

There once was a young woman. She was new to the big city and was attending a downtown church for the first time in her life. She had been coming for several months and had become an active part of the youth group. She always drove the same way to church. One Sunday, she was forced to take a detour because of construction. The neighborhoods she drove through were very different from those where she lived. There were no big houses or pretty lawns anywhere. Instead, there were shabby shacks, yards full of trash, and people who looked sad and desperate. That night, the young woman described her drive to the youth group and told them how upset she had been. She told the group she wanted to help but didn't know how. Someone in the group said, "Just go another way. Then you won't see it."

All of us, if we're honest, have had thoughts like that. If we don't see things or face issues, then we don't have to deal with them. If we don't see the poor, the outcasts, or the sick, then we don't have to include them in our lives. It is much like the Pharisees of Jesus' day. They stayed clear of the outcasts, considering them to be *am ha-aretz,* or undesirables. Then along came Jesus, who changed everything.

As soon as Jesus began his ministry, he spent time with people who were considered to be outsiders. He called fishermen and tax collectors to be his disciples. He ate with sinners, and he healed lepers. He spent time with prostitutes. Jesus fed the poor, healed the sick, and ministered to the outcasts. He also ministered to the rich, but as he did so, he continually called them to be compassionate and to care for the poor and needy.

What does it mean for us? If we are walking in Jesus' footsteps, then we are called to live as he did. Jesus calls us to care for sinners, outcasts, and the poor.

Are you intentionally building relationships with the kinds of people Jesus befriended? Are you connecting with people outside the church? Are you allowing them to see the love of God shining through you? That's what Jesus did. . . . Jesus went to the outsiders, befriended them, and sought to draw them to God, not by judgment but by love.
—From *The Way: Walking in the Footsteps of Jesus*, by Adam Hamilton

# Exploring the Lesson

## *Biblical Foundation*

[Jesus] left Judea and started back to Galilee. But he had to go through Samaria. So he came to a Samaritan city called Sychar, near the plot of ground that Jacob had given to his son Joseph. Jacob's well was there, and Jesus, tired out by his journey, was sitting by the well. It was about noon. A Samaritan woman came to draw water, and Jesus said to her, "Give me a drink." (His disciples had gone to the city to buy food.) The Samaritan woman said to him, "How is it that you, a Jew, ask a drink of me, a woman of Samaria?" (Jews do not share things in common with Samaritans.) Jesus answered her, "If you knew the gift of God, and who it is that is saying to you, 'Give me a drink,' you would have asked him, and he would have given you living water." (John 4:3-10 NRSV)

51

## *Video Presentation and Discussion (Optional)*

On the DVD, watch Session 5: Sinners, Outcasts, and the Poor.

SIGHTS
- The ruins of the town of Kursi
- Jacob's Well

INSIGHTS

In Kursi, Jesus cast out demons from a man who had been ostracized by society and lived among the graves in the cemetery. When Jesus commanded the demons to leave the man, they entered the swine and jumped off a cliff. The man himself was so grateful that he shared the good news to all around him and became the first missionary to the Gentiles.

- In Jesus' time, what do you think it meant to be possessed by demons? How did the man respond when Jesus healed him?
- What demons do we face today? How do you think we should deal with them?

The Samaritans were outcasts and enemies of the Jews, yet Jesus went through Samaria and spent time with them. There, he met a woman at the well and talked to her about her life. She was considered undesirable—she had been married and divorced five times and was living with a man who was not her husband. Nonetheless, Jesus offered her grace and forgiveness. She became the first missionary to the Samaritans.

- How has Jesus come into your life? In what ways has your experience been similar to that of the woman at the well?
- How can you be a missionary where you live?

## *Bringing the Scripture to My Life*

Jesus visited unlikely places and cared for different sorts of people during his ministry. He kept company with nobodies, the people who didn't count. To paraphrase a popular song, Jesus hung out with people in low places.

- What do Jesus' actions tell us about our own lives?
- Who do you spend time with? Why?
- Who, if anyone, do you show love to without showing judgment? How could you do a better job of showing love?
- In what ways have you pushed others away? In what ways have you held others close?

Time after time, Luke's Gospel shows Jesus spending time with outcasts, breaking bread with sinners.

—From *The Way: Walking in the Footsteps of Jesus*, by Adam Hamilton

## *Going Deeper in Truth*

Read Luke 5:12-13 (CEB)

Jesus was in one of the towns where there was also a man covered with a skin disease. When he saw Jesus, he fell on his face and begged, "Lord, if you want, you can make me clean." Jesus reached out his hand, touched him, and said, "I do want to. Be clean." Instantly, the skin disease left him.

- What did it mean for the man with leprosy to be made clean?
- Who do you think needs healing in the world around you?

Read Luke 14:13-14 (CEB)

"Instead, when you give a banquet, invite the poor, crippled, lame, and blind. And you will be blessed because they can't repay you. Instead, you will be repaid when the just are resurrected."

- Who would you invite to such a dinner?
- What does it mean to be repaid when the just are resurrected?

Read 1 Corinthians 16:13-14 (CEB)

Stay awake, stand firm in your faith, be brave, be strong. Everything should be done in love.

- In what circumstances might our faith require us to be brave and strong?
- What do you think the writer means by doing things in love? When do you do things in love? When don't you?

## Experiencing Life in Community

### RICE DINNER

Gather the group for a meal. Have the group sit on the floor. Pass out small bowls of cooked white rice and small cups of water. Talk about how this is the type of meal that the majority of the poor in the world get to eat, if they are lucky. Talk about hunger in the world and what followers of Jesus can do to help feed the hungry.

### SAMARITAN THEATER

As a group, read Luke 10:25-37, the parable of the Good Samaritan. Assign each person a character in the story, and then have the group act out the story. Afterward discuss how it felt to be those characters. Brainstorm ways to be a "Good Samaritan" this week.

## *Making It Personal*

Here are two ways to put what you've learned into action in the coming week and beyond:

1. Think about the hungry in your community. Skip one meal (or snack) this week and donate the money saved to your local food bank. Pray for those who are hungry every day.

2. Look for someone in your daily life who is considered an outcast. It may be someone at school who is ignored or made fun of; it may be someone who is very sick; it may be someone who has done something bad. Think of ways to let that person know that Jesus loves him or her. Choose one thing to do for that person, and then do it.

# Wrapping Up

## *Listening for God*

Gather in a prayer circle. Ask each person, as part of the prayer, to name a category of people (not individual names) who are social outcasts, such as the homeless or those with AIDS. After each group is named, pray together, "Lord help me to be your hands and feet to these, my brothers and sisters." After all have prayed, close with the following prayer:

*O God, you moved among us and taught us how to live. May we faithfully walk in your footsteps and care for the least of those around us. Amen.*

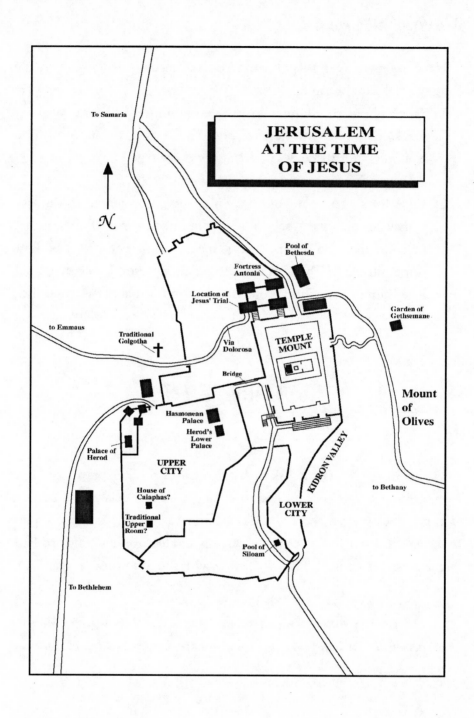

JERUSALEM
AT THE TIME
OF JESUS

To Samaria

N

Pool of
Bethesda

Fortress
Antonia

Location of
Jesus' Trial

Garden of
Gethsemane

to Emmaus

Traditional
Golgotha

Via
Dolorosa

TEMPLE
MOUNT

Bridge

Mount
of
Olives

Hasmonean
Palace

Herod's
Lower
Palace

KIDRON VALLEY

Palace of
Herod

UPPER
CITY

to Bethany

House of
Caiaphas?

LOWER
CITY

Traditional
Upper
Room?

Pool of
Siloam

To Bethlehem

# 6. The Final Week
## *Jerusalem*

## Getting Started

### *Goals for This Session*

—Examine the Gospel accounts of Jesus' last week of life.
—Understand that Jesus was a different kind of king, not what the world expected.
—Recognize that as followers of Jesus, we must realize the importance of Jesus' sacrifice on the cross.

### *Words to Know*

**Hosanna:** This Hebrew word is used to express adoration and praise.

***Patibulum:*** This Latin word refers to a horizontal beam for a cross of crucifixion.

# Introduction

Have you ever had something really good happen to you? You may have made the highest grade on a test, or one of your school sports teams may have become state champion. Things are going great, and then failure strikes. The school team, which was once state champ, is now lucky to win a single game. After receiving that high grade, you walk into your next class and learn about a pop quiz on the reading assignment you overlooked. Both triumph and failure seem to be parts of life.

Nobody knew this any better than Jesus, especially during his last week of life. Claiming to be the long-awaited Messiah, Jesus rode into the city on a royal animal. He entered Jerusalem to the shouts of *hosanna*. Everybody was excited. Things were going to be different and better. The Messiah had arrived.

Then things began to fall apart. The week quickly went from great to really bad. Through it all, Jesus showed us what greatness looks like. By washing his disciples' feet after the Last Supper, he demonstrated what it is to be a servant. And in giving his life, Jesus gave the greatest gift of all. At the end of the week he hung on a cross, apparently defeated. In the world's eyes he was a failure. But that wasn't the end of the story.

> During this, the final week of his life, Jesus would be hailed, however briefly, as a king. Yet the events that would follow made clear he was a very different kind of king than the crowds, and perhaps even his disciples, had hoped for. The crown he would wear was a crown of thorns. His enthronement would occur on a cross. As we ponder the events of that week, we ask: What kind of king is Jesus?"
>
> —From *The Way: Walking in the Footsteps of Jesus*, by Adam Hamilton

# Exploring the Lesson

## *Biblical Foundation*

They brought the colt to Jesus and threw their cloaks on it; and he sat on it. Many people spread their cloaks on the road, and others spread leafy branches that they had cut in the fields. Then those who went ahead and those who followed were shouting, "Hosanna! Blessed is the one who comes in the name of the Lord! Blessed is the coming kingdom of our ancestor David! Hosanna in the highest heaven!" (Mark 11:7-10 NRSV)

## *Video Presentation and Discussion (Optional)*

On the DVD, watch Session 6: The Final Week.

### SIGHTS

- The Temple Mount is where Jesus taught.
- The Mount of Olives is where Jesus triumphantly entered the city of Jerusalem on Palm or Passion Sunday
- The Garden of Gethsemane is where Jesus went to pray on his last night and where he was betrayed.
- The Via Dolorosa is the path where it is believed Jesus carried the *patibulum,* the horizontal bar of his cross, from the place of his trial to his place of death.
- The Church of the Holy Sepulchre sits above where Jesus is believed to have been crucified and buried.

## INSIGHTS

- Jesus' last week was very full. The places and events of that week are important and have always been important to Christians. Watching the video, we can imagine Jesus in some of these places during his final week.
- Is it important to think about the last places Jesus was alive on this earth? Why or why not?
- Where did Jesus go that final week, and what did he do in each place?

## *Bringing the Scripture to My Life*

Jesus not only taught us how to live, but he showed us as well. He demonstrated how to be faithful and how to be a servant.

- What did Jesus do in his final week to show us how to be a servant?
- What does it mean in today's world to be a servant?

This is the kind of King we follow, a king whose standard is the cross. Many look at the cross and see Christ's suffering and death for them, a "full and perfect sacrifice for the sins of the world," and indeed this is one of the profound and powerful truths of the cross. But there is more. When I look at the cross, I see a divine love story centered on a God who suffered to save the human race. This love is selfless and sacrificial, a parent dying for a child, a lover dying for the beloved. Ultimately, the cross is a sign of the lengths to which God will go to save us from our sin and brokenness. It reminds us that forgiveness came at a great price. Luke includes the words Jesus prayed from the cross, words that I find utterly astounding, a prayer transcending space and time, offered on Calvary for all people everywhere: "Father, forgive them, they know not what they do."

—From *The Way: Walking in the Footsteps of Jesus,* by Adam Hamilton

## Going Deeper in Truth

Read Matthew 5:44 (CEB)

"But I say to you, love your enemies and pray for those who harass you."

- How did Jesus exemplify loving enemies and praying for them?
- What does loving your enemies look like?

Read Luke 22:42 (CEB)

He said, "Father, if it's your will, take this cup of suffering away from me. However, not my will but your will must be done."

- When you are experiencing difficult times, do you find it easy or hard to pray? Why?
- What can you gain by praying during difficult times?

## Experiencing Life in Community

### WRITE A SONG

Divide into groups. Take a tune that is familiar and write new words to it. The words should tell about Jesus' willingness to be a servant and how he wants you to be a servant. Those who feel comfortable doing so can take turns singing the song for the rest of the group.

### FOOT-WASHING SERVICE

If your group is open to it, celebrate a foot washing. The group sits in a circle with a bowl of water, and towels are passed around. Each person washes or dabs water on the feet of the person to his or her immediate right. As you participate in these actions, remember that Jesus washed the feet of his disciples.

## *Making It Personal*

Here are two ways to put what you've learned into action in the coming week and beyond:

1. Spend time thinking about the last week in the life of Jesus. Write some diary entries as if you had been with Jesus during that week. Describe what you saw and the feelings you had.

2. Write a statement of faith in Christ. The statement should be no more than three sentences, and it should succinctly state what Jesus has done for you and what he wants you to do.

# Wrapping Up

## *Listening for God*

Place a cross in the front of the room so you and all group members can see it. Gaze at the cross. Think about the final week of Jesus' life on earth. Ask someone to slowly read the last words of Jesus from the cross.

Father, forgive them for they know not what they do.
Behold your mother, behold your son.
My God, my God, why have you forsaken me?
I thirst.
Into your hands I commend my spirit.
It is finished.

After the words are read, sit quietly praying, and then leave the room in silence.

I have been senior pastor of the Church of the Resurrection for over two decades. Every year I end my Easter sermon the same way. I mention that people ask me from time to time, "Do you really believe this stuff? You're a smart guy. Do you really believe that Jesus rose from the dead?"

My response is always the same: "I not only believe it; I'm counting on it."

—From *The Way: Walking in the Footsteps of Jesus,*
   by Adam Hamilton

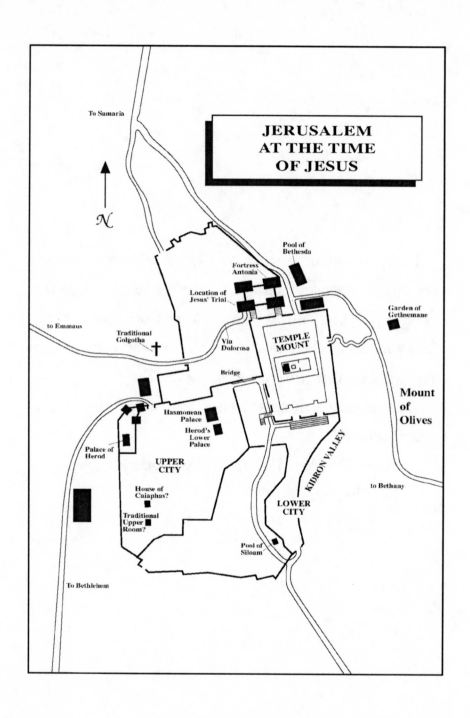

JERUSALEM
AT THE TIME
OF JESUS

To Samaria

N

Pool of
Bethesda

Fortress
Antonia

Location of
Jesus' Trial

Garden of
Gethsemane

to Emmaus

Traditional
Golgotha

Via
Dolorosa

TEMPLE
MOUNT

Bridge

Mount
of
Olives

Hasmonean
Palace

Herod's
Lower
Palace

Palace of
Herod

UPPER
CITY

KIDRON VALLEY

House of
Caiaphas?

LOWER
CITY

to Bethany

Traditional
Upper
Room?

Pool of
Siloam

To Bethlehem

# Epilogue
## *Your Defining Story*

---

## Note

*The Way: Walking in the Footsteps of Jesus* is a six-week study, but the study, like the book on which it is based, also includes an epilogue about the Resurrection, titled "Your Defining Story." Groups using *The Way* as a Lenten study thus have the option of a session for Easter Sunday, and groups using the study at other times of year have the option of extending it to seven weeks. In the book, the DVD, and this youth edition, the epilogue uses an abbreviated format.

## Getting Started

### *Goals for This Session*
—Begin to examine personal identity and the story or stories on which it is based.
—Understand that the Resurrection is the defining story for Christians.
—Recognize that Jesus loves, forgives, and calls his followers to serve.

## Words to Know

**Resurrection:** This word means to return to life from death.

**Chaos:** This word means complete confusion or disorder.

## Introduction

Who are you? What makes you . . . you? Think about words that define you: son, daughter, sibling, grandchild, athlete, band member, cheerleader, gamer, loner. There are so many words that describe who you are and what you do. Make a list of them. Examine that list. Does your list include words such as *Christian* or *disciple*? As Christians we are defined by words that indicate that we walk in the footsteps of Jesus.

But words are not the only way you are defined. Another part of your identity is the story of who you are. There are the stories of your family, of your childhood, of your teenage years. And as a Christian you are defined by the story of the Resurrection. That is the most important story of all.

The Resurrection means that the crucifixion was not the end of the story but the beginning. It is the answer to the loss of hope on that Good Friday and to the loss of hope in the world.

Because of the Resurrection, we know that even in the midst of sorrow, Jesus is with us and will see us through. We can have confidence that sorrow and suffering are not the end of the story. In the Resurrection, Jesus also brought forgiveness. Even his closest disciples denied knowing him and ran away. And yet he forgave them. What freedom and joy that brings to the world!

Bad things happen in this messed-up and chaotic world. But the chaos of life is just the first part of the Christian story. The rest of the story is the Resurrection. When Jesus died and rose from the dead, he changed the story forever. He changed your story.

The cross leads me to gratitude and awe. It leads me to a love of Christ and a deep desire to follow him and live for him. I want to walk in his footsteps. I want to live as a citizen of his Kingdom. I want to love as he loved. I want to practice his way.

—From *The Way: Walking in the Footsteps of Jesus*, by Adam Hamilton

# Exploring the Lesson

## Biblical Foundation

When it was evening on that day, the first day of the week, and the doors of the house where the disciples had met were locked for fear of the Jews, Jesus came and stood among them and said, "Peace be with you." After he said this, he showed them his hands and his side. Then the disciples rejoiced when they saw the Lord. Jesus said to them again, "Peace be with you. As the Father has sent me, so I send you." When he had said this, he breathed on them and said to them, "Receive the Holy Spirit. If you forgive the sins of any, they are forgiven them; if you retain the sins of any, they are retained." (John 20:19-23 NRSV)

## Bringing the Scripture to My Life

Jesus' death and Resurrection are the defining highlights of the Christian story. The Church of the Holy Sepulchre reminds us of both the pain of the crucifixion and the joy of the Resurrection. In the pain of the crucifixion we see the pain of the world; in the joy of the Resurrection we find our hope and joy.

- How did the disciples feel after Jesus' crucifixion? How did they feel when they finally realized he had risen?
- What do Jesus' death and Resurrection mean in your life? Why?

In the "angel stone," found in the tomb beneath the Church of the Holy Sepulchre, we are reminded of the stone that was rolled away from Jesus' tomb. The stone, Adam Hamilton reminds us, was not rolled away for Jesus but for humanity, so that all could know that Jesus' body was not there, that he had been raised from the dead.

- How does reading and hearing about the place where Jesus may have been crucified and resurrected make you feel? Why?
- If you traveled to the Holy Land, what are some of the places you would like to see?

## Going Deeper in Truth

Read 1 Peter 1:3 (CEB)

May the God and Father of our Lord Jesus Christ be blessed! On account of his vast mercy, he has given us new birth. You have been born anew into a living hope through the resurrection of Jesus Christ from the dead.

- What does it mean to have a living hope?
- What does having a living hope mean for your life?

Read Romans 12:6-8a (CEB)

We have different gifts that are consistent with God's grace that has been given to us. If your gift is prophecy, you should prophesy in proportion to your faith. If your gift is service, devote yourself to serving. If your gift is teaching, devote yourself to teaching. If your gift is encouragement, devote yourself to encouraging.

- God has given all of us gifts with which to share the good news. What gifts have you been given?
- How are you using your gifts to serve and to glorify God?

## Experiencing Life in Community

### LIVING PHOTOGRAPHY

Divide into teams. Each team is to design three "living pictures" that represent Jesus' Resurrection. The team must stage these pictures in real time, using every person. Teams will share their pictures by asking the large group to close their eyes, then arranging the picture, then asking the group to open their eyes again. This process will continue for all three photos of each team. Afterward, discuss how the different pictures captured the joy and the excitement of the Resurrection.

## *Making It Personal*

Here are two ways to put what you've learned into action in the coming week and beyond:

1. Make a poster for your home that shows the joy of the Resurrection in your life. Spend time thinking about what the poster should include. When it is complete, hang it on the wall. Use it daily as a reminder of the wonderful gift that Jesus has given you.

2. Make a list of all the ways that you can walk in the footsteps of Jesus. Choose a specific action for each day of the week, and then do it.

# Wrapping Up

## *Listening for God*

Sit together as a group. Think about the story of Jesus and about the importance of walking in his footsteps. Then pray this prayer together:

*Dear God, thank you for loving us so much that you sent Jesus. Thank you for the fact that he came to earth and lived as one of us. Thank you for the most awesome gift of the Resurrection. Help us to walk in Jesus' footsteps, today and always. Amen.*

# Churchwide Study
# of *The Way*

*The Way: Walking in the Footsteps of Jesus* explores the life and ministry of Jesus Christ. Author Adam Hamilton leads readers through the places Jesus' ministry took place, explains the culture of Bible times, and explores what it means to live as followers of Jesus.

A churchwide study program for all ages will help people come to a deeper understanding of what it means to live as Jesus' followers and will invite families to learn about Jesus together. The program will offer opportunities for learning, for intergenerational projects and activities, and for reaching out in service to the community.

## *Resources for the Churchwide Study*

Adults
*The Way: Walking in the Footsteps of Jesus*—Book
*The Way: DVD with Leader Guide* (Optional for youth)
*The Way: 40 Days of Reflection*—Devotional Companion

Youth
*The Way: Youth Study Edition*

Children
*The Way: Children's Leader Guide*

## Schedule

Many churches have weeknight programs that include an evening meal; an intergenerational gathering time; and classes for children, youth, and adults. The following schedule illustrates one way to organize a weeknight program.

5:30 p.m.  Meal

6:00 p.m.  Intergenerational gathering introducing weekly themes and places for the lesson. This time may include presentations, skits, music, and opening or closing prayers.

6:15 p.m.–8:15 p.m.  Classes for children, youth, and adults

Alternatively, churches may want to do this study as a Sunday school program. This setting would be similar to the weeknight setting. The following schedule takes into account a shorter class time, which is the norm for Sunday morning programs.

10 minutes  Intergenerational gathering
45 minutes  Classes for children, youth, and adults

Choose a schedule that works best for your congregation and its Christian education programs.

## *Activity Suggestions*

### FOLLOW JESUS BY SERVING! CHURCHWIDE SERVICE DAY

An important part of following Jesus is being the hands and feet of Jesus in today's world. A churchwide service day would be a good kick-off or wrap-up event. Plan multiple service opportunities for the day, choosing some projects appropriate for each age level. If your church has a missions committee, check with them for ideas. Consult with local service agencies to see if there are projects you could do for them.

### COLLECTION DRIVE

In conjunction with your churchwide service day or separately, use this study as an opportunity to collect items for donation to a local service organization. Possible ideas include food for the local food pantry, monetary donations for any number of organizations, children's books for a hospital library or school, baby supplies for a shelter, or school supplies for an elementary school.

CPSIA information can be obtained at www.ICGtesting.com
Printed in the USA
LVOW08s2102290114

371505LV00002B/3/P